An Infinite Affliction of Words

ERIKA STORM

Hardback ISBN 978-1-0688725-0-1
Ebook ISBN 978-1-0688725-2-5
Paperback ISBN 978-1-0688725-1-8

Typeset in Dreaming Outloud Pro and London

Edited by Birgitte Maarup

Photography by Kadin Kryski

DEDICATION

TGK
My solid safe

I KNOW THIS FEELS SCARY,
AND THAT IS OKAY
BECAUSE I AM SAFE

I Loved a Lying Person

I took off my rings as he put his on. As I was taking mine off, and mother-in-law's hawk-like eyes were fixating on the empty finger, he put his on to signify that he was not done. I was.

I had been wearing mine for 5.5 years – proudly – and his had been lying odd places around the house even when he was able to wear it because it was no longer a work hazard.

I was done. I am done. And yet I keep going back and forth. This is not heartbreak; it is not just a marriage in dissolution.

We are lucky to be alive. My fingers are empty. There are no emojis to his name in my phone book, and his ICE nomination in my phone has been reallocated.

What happened was not so bad, was it? It was much, much worse. We are in every sense for every purpose lucky to be alive.

Still I keep going back and forth because in that moment he can be that perfect partner, but only if I sacrifice everything that is me. I am not willing to do that, and I am not willing to let the kids live in an environment where they need to make themselves smaller.

So how do I untangle my brain? I feel like I have been brainwashed. I can read the words in his mental health notes. I can understand them, I know what they mean, and I cannot comprehend them in the context of this person. I can objectively acknowledge that I have done the right thing, such a right thing, to remove the kids from such a person, but I could have dealt with it, could I not?

I loved an unpredictable person unable to feel empathy or sympathy for others. I loved a lying person.

Here is the thing, though. I love myself more. I love myself, and this kind of love does not come with strings attached or conditions that are meant to be unconditional. I just need to figure out who I am.

Maybe

He tried to kill himself because I left him; and, in an attempt to keep myself safe, served him with court orders. My effort to tell the truth in the affidavit made him off himself, and I feel like a bully.

It feels as though I made him - or forced him - to make an attempt at his own life, and rather than being a witness or bystander, it is as if I almost put the cord around his neck. It feels like an impossible mission to go beyond this and truly separate myself from him due to this event.

It created both a distance and intense fear of a repeat, and it has made me almost bend over backwards in an effort to profusely apologize and attempt to assume as little responsibility for the actions and events leading up to his attempt.

If I just had not said anything, or left, or gone to the lawyer, maybe everything would still be fine.

Rewired

I stare at you
through the pain inflicted
through the trauma
that you dealt so freely

I stare at a life
across oceans and continents
a life becoming dust
just a little bit
with new breaths

I stare at you
a father
with no children
a storyteller with no truths
a husband
with no wife
a human being
who took his own breath

I look at me
try to desperately
to find the me
in me
with remnants
and memories
who I were, what I am
so rewired
by your violations
so rewired
by your transgressions

I almost lost so much more
I almost lost everything
you almost took my breath away
you almost did

But I breathe still
I see your lies
so rewired

no longer under your thumb
maybe even reborn
so truly unexpected
a new kind of beauty
a foreign kind of freedom knocked

More than deserved
sheer coincidences and unrealized
emotions were reciprocated

A new kind of acceptance
a new kind of incomparable

A crush turning to
a new kind of beautiful fall
backwards and forwards
into myself

Keep You Safe

I gave life and almost lost my own
I gave you air, and you take mine away

In the late hours of the night
I became a mother
blood flowed from me and into you and onto
the hospital bed, out of me
and I felt my mind grow hazy
I felt myself slipping away
bluey after bluey after bluey
I was safe in their hands
and my hands were too weak to hold you

With no help I learned your noises and cries
knees weak from my dance with Death
I had to stand
so I stood
and I fed you with my body

My body that had protected you
carried you, nurtured you
and you were no longer safe
because half of you lost its mind
I was paralyzed as you came close to not being
as you came too close to being removed
as I had to leave you with the half of you
that had lost its mind

From the ashes into the fire
did you learn to walk on hot coals
maybe your voice was stolen
when you knew you would not be heard

I gave you a home in my womb
In my arms
yet I never realized the trauma
I carried from the night you became
struggling and yet intuitively
mothering and nurturing
I felt numb

there was no chance to revel, to stop, to love, to be
constantly putting out fires
constantly fixing and putting in order
constantly putting myself last
constantly sacrificing my mind, myself, my worth
my identity, me
for the half of you having gone insane
to keep you safe from harm

But it put you in harm's way
in saving you I lost myself
and I was told I was lesser for it
that as a mother I was unfit, unready, useless
prioritizing wrongly

Leading us to freedom I dissolved
triggered by your actions
I carried guilt and shame
and I tried to find space
hold space with grace
and you kept pushing, keep on pushing me
closer to what feels like the edge
and I try to hold space to gently guide you
through this space
navigating safety
while each day I see features in you
that have not lost their mind
and yet still clearly came from the part of you
that lost its mind
I know where you came from
I nurtured you
my heartbeat was your lullaby
my body fed you
I know where you come from

Unrecognizable

He stole my words
and you feed them back to me
kiss me, breathe my air
feel me wake

He stole my mind
my brain is damaged
unrecognizable in my own eyes
I do not know the person in the mirror
and somehow you know me
I am recognizable in your eyes
I am found

He stole my free will
and you offer options, possibilities
conversations, questions, adoration
hold me tight
warm my body
feel me quiver
as I remember what confidence feels like

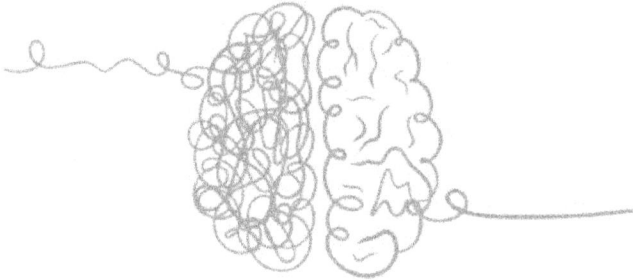

Tiny Plurals

You bring me roses
and talk of winters
winters in the plural
watching the snow fall cuddled into you

You meet me where I am
and while I protect smaller beings
I place trust in you protecting me
I let go in your arms

Unexpectedly mine
wholly yours
we weave through heavy and light
without effort

You are never far away
yet absence makes my being ache
to feel you close
feels like being complete

I guess perhaps
maybe I love you
just in a tiny way
like I have never known love
or to love before

Unexpectedly, consistently
I love you

Warp-speed

Not regulated
not dysregulated
in a wasteland of triggers

Emotional tide waves rolling off you
uncertainty, trepidation
tip-toe, tip-toe, tip-toe
I am caught in the slip
carried further out to sea
caught in the undertow of something
I do and do not understand

At the slowest warp-speed
I let my fingers memorize your body
commit your face to memory
I do not want to forget you

I feel you, see you, hear you, miss you
want more seconds in my minutes with you
your emotional wake sucks me in
and makes me want to run
stick my head in the sand
not deal because I sense you so clear

And you will not hear me begging
I will not beg you to stay
and still I am in the potential
not kissing your soft lips ever again
would be hard

The potential of us
full stop
not just a reckless love

Twin Flames

My skin is a golden web
like rings in water
marked by your fingertips
anticipating and moving with each touch

Like waves rolling in
you leave me out of breath
across a remote galaxy
a sweet release when it is caught
and let go of

Definitely not nothing
an unshakeable feeling
so intense, so magnetic
you draw me in
and I long to be in your presence
every touch, soft lips on mine
promising and still silent

Not soul mates
not nothing
yet also not soul bound
unequivocally, consistently, unimaginable
from the first moment
perhaps I wanted you
for months and before the new year came to

A sense of peace, belonging, authenticity, synchronicity
you mirrored onto me and I onto you
I feel found not even knowing
I was lost
I feel homebound not even knowing
I was way bound

A sense of belonging
willingly, freely, adoringly, consistently
I love you
just a tiny bit
who would have guessed

Like two halves becoming whole
neither aware that either existed
not soul mates
definitely more

We got swallowed by the waves
never put out, never not hungry, never not longing
like twin flames
burning together and apart
free to choose
like there ever was a choice

Connected

For all my words I have none
no words
in any language which sufficiently describe
what I feel

Because "I love you" feels transcendable
in time with time
I am so proud
you call me "mine"

and I have no words
with you I feel at home
and my body longs for our connection
I do not know
I usually do and I have never felt
what I now feel

I have never felt
what I now feel

And I have never felt so whole
I knew I was never truly broken
I just had no idea
I never knew that another person
could bring another whole
new whole outside of my own

I know that for our unlikely meeting
that for our strongest connection
somehow there is no doubt
and looking at you across the kitchen
I catch myself thinking
that I would do this lifetime after lifetime
I catch myself thinking
how in love with you I am

And for all my lost words
you are the one I want
today, tomorrow, ten years from now

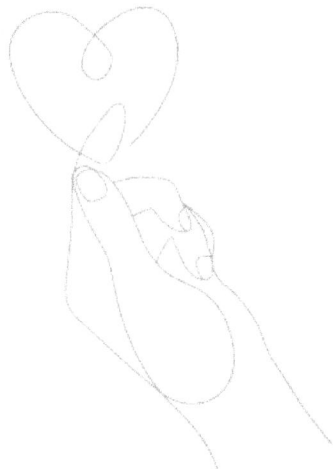

Alexandra

A year ago, I knew that my days in New Zealand were numbered. I was counting down, mentally crossing them out as I got up each morning. Another day gone. 75 days. 10 weeks and 5 days. 1800 hours.

I had never imagined that those 75 days would be so transformative, so definitive.

21 days gone and I flew to Alexandra to say goodbye. Or maybe it was see you later. I do not know. It felt more final than just see you later, and the amount of tears shed would be a testament to something else.
I remember getting off the plane in Queenstown and feeling my lungs get that first hit of 4 degrees cold air.
It felt like waking from a deep slumber, and perhaps this was the first step back towards myself. I made sure to breathe all that frosty air for as long as I was in Alexandra, and when I left, I knew I was done.

What transpired through the next 49 days, I do not believe anyone could have predicted. It was traumatizing and terrible, and it is something I should never have had to witness or deal with.
With 44 days to go, I took my wedding band off. I came to New Zealand married with no children, and I would be leaving New Zealand single with two children.
There was no doubt in my mind, I had to leave. I had to leave the country. There was no other choice if I was to have a future.

New Zealand changed me in many ways, and there are many reasons why I should not be smiling. There are many reasons why I should not be standing my 5'2" tall, and yet I am. There are many reasons, and I did not deserve a single one of them, however, I am coming to embrace the growth that is a result of those reasons.

A year ago my days were numbered, and now they are not. What a curious feeling.

HALFWAY AND NOWHERE NEAR

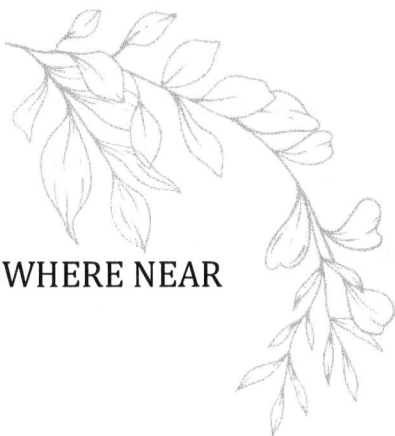

Slowly Becoming

It is like looking at the world through a looking glass. I see myself consciously with effort, removing myself from what I was, what I could be. I set a full stop, I keep turning the pages.

In your arms I find the eye of the storm – I find the I in the storm that ravaged my life for so long. Standing at the edge looking at and past the river, seeing the world for what it is, what it was, and what it will be knowing that for a split second I had stopped moving. The absolute peace and tranquil on our side of the river, bringing time to a halt, simultaneous with the rushed speed mere meters away.

Everything can and will co-exist. I am more than my trauma. I am more. As I continue to reinforce this concept, I become tangible to myself; I step through the looking glass and into myself.

I am slowly becoming. I moved heaven and earth to find freedom, I was Atlas for just a little while, and I am understanding that I do not have to carry the world on my shoulders.

I am no longer alone, seeing myself through your eyes adds a new layer. A new layer wanting to explore the juxtaposition of this world, where it feels safe to pursue more tranquil moments in the middle of the storm.

I am okay.

Adrenaline

Removed hostility radiating off you
in waves unmatching your heartbeat

So fast I hear it in your chest
flooded by adrenaline coursing through your system

You are ice on the outside
a stone wall shut down, shut off

And I feel you with my tiny frame
desperately seeking your arms around me
a full on embrace to compress my nervous system
to regulate what I feel becoming lost and loose
dysregulated

Perhaps I was the most regulated
your lips seeking mine
as though you were looking to know
that I was still there

Dancing With Death

And as I stood there, I realized I did not want to die. I had too much life, it was too premature. Strangely enough, the realization was stark and prominent and traumatizing. Perhaps even more than the violence and abuse.
That something was taken from me. Robbed. Stolen. Misused. Beaten out of me.
And I did not see that I was always at risk. That dancing with Death could form such a mind break.

Constant

Maybe it is not everything that needs talking about

Maybe it is not everything that needs to bear a word

Maybe some things are
Maybe some things just be

And that is a constant in itself

Like you
And me

Always Near

I want to ask where you were all my life
and I already know

I was out and about
I was busy getting lost in continents
I was busy losing my dreams and a sense of self

I want to ask where you were
and I already know

Because I was nowhere close
I was nowhere near

So I ask rhetorically
because I already know you were far away
'till you were not

And I already know
that kilometers and meters do not matter
because I was removed
and I was so far away
even though you were always near

I want to ask
and I already know
I had to be ready to fall in love with you
and myself

All at once
and now you are in my heart
held so closely in my arms

Trust Fall

It is a trust fall falling into myself
realizing I am self-made, self-helped
that I survived

It is a trust fall falling forward and backwards
stumbling in bewilderment at what I accomplished
intercontinental moves, a Forbes article, a business
all before 30

It is a trust fall jumping into the unknown
not realizing the potential others see
and still choosing to trust them
place trust in what is reflected

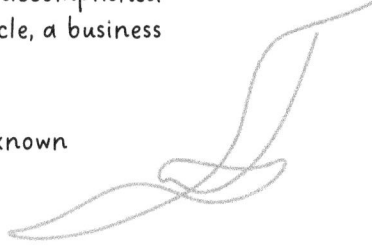

It is a trust fall placing trust in myself

Frustration

I know it does not matter. And I still feel the sting and burn of unjust tears from pure frustration. I had so hoped for a full week next to you, being able to touch you as I fall asleep, kissing you as the first thing before we are fully awake.

Feeling more safe than I have in years, knowing in my soul that I am home, that I have found where I belong. And despite knowing that the services required for this full week to happen are unreliable, I still hope, and I hope so much I left things at your place.

I know it does not matter because we will get our three nights another time. And you will be coming home to me on a different set of three nights.

Here is the thing, though. I want to be next to you every single night. I want to no longer be dependent and reliable on unreliable services in order to be with you.

I want you to be my everyday-treat and wake up next to you every day. I long for the day you are no longer just a once-in-a-while-treat.

Confusion

I was/am hurt by ~~how you~~ what was said on Saturday

I am worried we will never be ready together

I want us to work towards being ready together

I feel that you could be/may be my full stop

I had hoped things had progressed since our last conversation

I want to sure you feel you are loved and respected, so when would be a good time to talk again?

I know my brain works quickly, and I can see that your pace is different

I am worried you may still be looking for red flags in me

I am feeling confused ~~when~~ because I know you are careful with your words, and I hear you say "when we go to Europe" with ease, and then "if we ever move in together"

I am worried that I trigger something in you based on your reaction the last two times we surfaced the conversation

AN INFINITE AFFLICTION OF WORDS

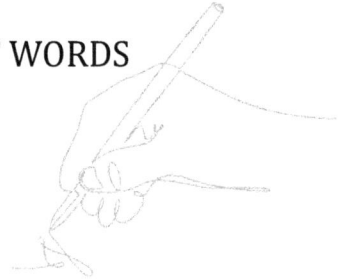

Seasons

My fingers are perpetually cold, never really seeking warmth and always letting it go as easily as it was found. I could write a book. I should write a book, and I do not know what I would write about. It feels like I have not written in months, and perhaps I have not.

It is not that words left me because I had figments and fragments and words and phrases in front of my eyes. I had starts and middle parts floating in front of me, getting lost and found in my brain, and never fully sticking for more than a mere moment. I do not know where August went. One moment I glance back and it is mid-October, and soon the snow is going to fall. It was just 32 degrees.

It is like lightning speed, and each day feels too short and yet like I have known you years. Years stacking on years. Towers of years and crumbling at the single digit months. So long. So far in such a short time. Lost and all of a sudden oh so very found. At home in a foreign city. Semi-familiar roads light up and become part of the puzzle. Part of a world, a reality manifesting beyond the reach of imagination.

The happenstance. The odds. An affliction of acronyms and antonyms. Never synonymous. Is it that my pen would spill my emotions in front of my eyes? Letting me know that my afflicted days were soon to be a chapter shut; that happiness is true and real? That I was never so found as when in your arms? Is it that I have no words? Because my hand does its own thing, and all I do is watch.
Is it that loving you feels monumental; monumentally infinite? Yet. There is a time for everything. Yet. And I want you in the past, present and future tense.

12 months ago I had no idea you existed. I had no idea that a love like you existed. The stuff of fairytales. The stuff of books I longingly read, the pages I devoured. You feel so close and yet so far away. A consistent part of my life; you are like coming up for fresh air when all I did was scream under water.
You take my pain and turn it into pleasure. Making me hungry for so much more.

Apparently it was you. Maybe I was meant to find you. Apparently it was you. You that I was meant to love and dream of a life with. Maybe it was always you.
I just did not know.

Puzzle Pieces

It is almost time
it is almost time for everything to turn white
the first snowfall
where did time go

I step out
look at my tracks
I have walked so far, so far for so long

Until it made sense
and I look at the sky at the stars blinking
maybe I have got stardust in my eyes
and cotton candy on my lips

I fall back onto myself
into and off myself

And I feel your hand in mine
so foreign and home all at once
and I feel the weight of its support
your support at every turn

And I look at who I have become
who I am becoming
and I fall into myself
in love with myself

Prone on my bed my hand reaches for yours
snow falls quietly
winter in bed with you
as I fall further trusting you more
infinitely accepting of everything you offer
and bring me

Never thought I would ever feel put back together
my missing piece

Triggered

Being triggered is me not being myself. It is my brain making sure I survive. I am so far into my recovery – still at the very beginning, and yet no longer at the start line that I know more. I know myself better, I am allowing myself grace to take the time.

So I felt my feelings towards you being boxed away. Cognitively, intellectually being pushed away for my brain to allow survival to reign. And I recognized this, and I knew it was in part from being triggered by you.

And so you apologized, even though the trigger is from me. I trust you. It is a different level of trust, one I did not even know existed. It is a trust that goes deeper and way further than just being nakedly comfortable with you. It means I feel I can rely on you; it means I will start to rely on you; it means I welcome your help, your presence, your being into my life.

And it feels terrifying. Because I thought I knew what love is, and my love for you is equally growing deeper and bigger.

I thought I was broken. I thought I was in a thousand pieces, and that I would spend my life picking up those pieces. And not once have you made me feel anything less than whole – or anything less than enough. And now I look at myself and wonder how this beautiful piece of kintsugi has happened in just six months.

I thought I was broken, unable to match, unable of being met, and you have shown me a world of wonder with every embrace.

So it felt like my feelings were being boxed away, and still instinctually, I knew that next to you was the only place I wanted to be. Having everything muffled and hazed out in survival feels miserable and horrible.

Realizing I trust you is so very daunting. I could choose to walk away, I could choose to remain so fiercely independent, and yet I choose you. From the moment I wake up 'till the moment I go to sleep, and every moment in between.

It also really means I would not be okay with not having you. I would survive, I would figure it out because I always do, and it is not a reality I would like to wake up to.

Being triggered, to me, now means that I will be waiting for my light bulb moment if I am aware that I am triggered. Obviously, I am currently very aware, and I know I have abandonment issues.

Moving countries as I have and being fine that way is either incredibly brave or bravery coming from abandonment trauma. I would rather be alone than rely on anyone because everyone else has without fault let me down.

Until I met you. With your steady consistency, your predictability, your space for me.

There is not a single thing more in my life that I can control since meeting you, and I am strangely okay with dealing with that now.

Because I know I can rely on your support, and on you. And so you keep mentioning sustainability, and that it is on your mind whether our solid communication, space, love and affection for each other is sustainable. You mention your careful, hesitant resistance because you are afraid of being hurt again, afraid of carrying the world on your shoulders only to be let down and left with naught, and that you need more time.

And I often wonder. Our baggage is similar, and so different, and yet so undeniably similar, and I was so quick to jump into the deep end.

And you caught me, you still do. I am just... there was and is something so different about you that never gave me the opportunity to not jump.

I do not want you to ever stop kissing me. And I am worried that for everything you are to me, maybe you are still terrified of being left with broken dreams at a perceived square one.

I am worried that I am not able to give or offer you what you so clearly give and offer me – a love, a level of respect, an imperfectly, unbroken me through your eyes. And I am worried if you in protecting yourself will never go beyond your careful resistance.

I said that you being all-in in would likely have been too much previously, and yet you know where I am. In. And I guess me trusting you would mean that I am also ready for that easing, if you are. I am worried if you will ever give me the opportunity to figuratively catch you, and that you would rather walk away.

I do not want to lose you. I do not mean to profess anything, I do not mean to declare anything; you just very simply feel like home, like I belong somewhere wholly and fully as me for the first time in my life. And for as comforting, as beautiful and amazing as it is, it is also equal amounts of terrifying to feel like you are the one, and when I told you, you walked away – maybe because the idea right now is so ludicrous.

Yet in my mind there is not a sliver of doubt. Time is letting me fall so much further for you, and I see myself state my needs for the first time ever. Trusting you is terrifying because I will not want you to let me down.

Layers

My sweet man
so ordinarily extraordinary in my eyes
so imperfectly perfect

I think I see you
with pasts so differently similar
so horribly wrong

I had never dreamed that yours was the face
I just could not forget
I had never imagined you becoming so much
when you first knocked on my door

They say trauma survivors speak a common language
and I feel so many layers between us
of attraction, lust, love, emotionality
of shared understanding

I feel you leaning in and pulling back
I feel you giving in and pulling away
because you were used

I feel your love hesitantly ready
carefully resisting
like your ghosts and skeletons do not want me there

Because the abuse carries strings
and you are only just starting to see them
my darling man
I am so sorry they left you no choice
I am so sorry you had to be so strong
my love

I feel that you are mine
I feel you should be for the rest of whatever
no infinities are long enough with you

I support you, love you, care for you
my handsome love
there is space for all of you with me

you do not have to be alone anymore

I am not going anywhere
I will not leave you
and you deserve to be free from your ghosts

No Words Left

I am still here, I am just finding my words.
I am still here, I still have words for you.

That is the point. I still have words for you.
Because it is becoming so clear that I have no words left for my own father. There are still words.

I just need more time.

Dissociation

I watch myself stumble and fall
as words not mine take over and replace
what I have fought to see
as dominoes I fall
fences down

As I fumble towards safety and regulation
I feel swamped by muchness
and I feel foreign words in my fingers
hot tears fill my eyes
as I trip myself over
retrace my steps and recede

Fighting between what I know and what I hear
and time disappears as I dissociate
unable to reach out
unable to find grounding
my brain shuts down and I
freeze

Remove my words
and let the juxtaposition float in front of my eyes
I see dominoes fall
I am dominoes
and I pretend I pivot
as the wave crushes the air from me

And I fight to come to
there is little sense
I know better and those words
still reigned
bringing with it a whole waterfall of despair

I could reach out
I could ask for a hand
I should ask for an anchor
and instead I shut down

For so long
my words were not my own

I had no words
my breaths were shallow as I survived
for so long I was looking through the glass
I did not pivot, I fell
the furthest in a while
back to wordlessness, worthlessness
for so long
I was a blank canvas
the ink in my heart still
and the pen gone from my finger

No more
I write my truth
my words are my voice
and I have a voice
and I am so terrified that my words are too many
that my voice is too much
and that I will be left
all alone again

182.5 Days

I know my little fixation on 6 months with you seems juvenile, and it kind of is. The first couple of relationships I ever had only lasted 6 months, so 6 months became this arbitrary timeline, measure in my mind for when relationships work or do not. Of course, that is a shitty way to measure or gauge anything because 6 months can be hardly any time at all, or it can be more. Infinitely more.

Truthfully, me saying "6 months" is probably a way for me to pinch myself that it is really *only* 6 months because it feels so much longer. Somehow being with you makes my days, months, seasons pass so fast. 6 months with you is 6 months of hugs, kisses, amazing love, no fights, open and honest communication. 6 months with you is still like coming up for fresh air, finding my footing, growing with you, supporting you and you me.

I think that is worth celebrating.

Screaming Under Water

Imagine if I had been listened to.
54 days ago.

Imagine if I had been listened to.
54 days ago.

36

EXPLOSIONS (INWARD)

On Fire

Highs and lows of a nervous system on fire
ebbs and flows as adrenaline set in

Fire and ice
all at once
highs and blows
nowhere safe

Highs and lows change to a steady flow
home at last
with a nervous system on fire
retracing and replacing
bored patience so slow

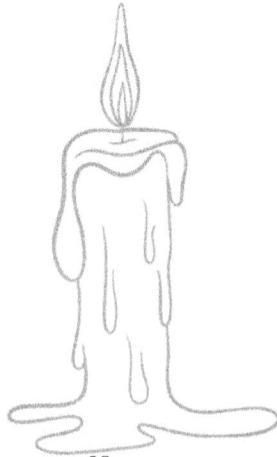

Atlas

He took my words
and he took my breath from my lips
the air from my lungs

Set me on fire with guilt and shame
carrying his world on my shoulders
I was Atlas for years

He took my words
he bound me with prickly thorns of false promises
into a marriage where love was replaced
with fists and each slap
and every bit of violence removed me
further from my words

He took me
and he moved and removed
in a toxic us against the world
I put out all his fires with my bare hands
stepped on the coals with bare feet
never good enough, never smart enough
always wrong

Volatility and disregard dominated
as I became his keeper
with no one to keep me

And now that I am finding my words
so safe in your arms
now with broken promises being undone
he claims he misses me
but how does one miss someone
they treated so badly

And as I soothe the burns on my hands
and as I now pursue my freedom
he tries to block it

And I see the manipulation
the lies

the inconsistencies
and the hubris

he threatened to kill me if I ever left him
he knows my address
because it is on the court documents
I need to disappear
into your arms
in a safe life with you

I need to be free

Wandering

He took my words
his dreams became mine
he took my money
200,000 to pursue peace

He bought me with false promises
he took my self-worth
sense of self with every word
mine turned against me

I became a wanderer in my own mind
forever grasping at strings I once knew
never finishing any race I started

He took my words
almost my life too
and now he claims he never did
and he continues to try and take my words
I am feeling crazy in my mind
because the abuse is not stopping
even half a world away

Contested

Like a bomb exploded
the lid was blown away
the dark crypt wide open

"I contest"
but he did it
"I did not treat (...) with mental and physical cruelty"
but he did
and I see the dominoes fall
like watching a train wreck
but he did
and I have no words I want to say

I wonder if in my mind
I was wrong
if in my mind
I made up stuff
and I find myself in a flashback
crossing an icy bridge
I feel my heart race in the night
as I listen for sounds while I sleep
I wake paralyzed from nightmares
and I know that I was true
to myself
and what happened to me

And I try to plan ahead
anticipate the next move
so I cover all my bases
with fallen rainforest

And find peace in your arms
the only place I can sleep

Courthouse

So many words
like pearls on a string

My mind is tired
needing sleep
gauging situations from a million angles
overthinking at a standstill

I stop and marvel
how such stillness, how such calm
how such quiet
and such longing
entered my life
how I so instinctually knew
so many words
tripping and falling
like a paradise lost

Sober in paradise feeling everything
and so much more
as the first tears spilled in a house of papers
crying through a connection

And it feels like labor all over
wave after wave except I bleed

Unsafe

No.

If only I could fall asleep in your arms tonight.

Little Love

I carried our love
in my womb

Between hibiscus and wild raspberry
under a blanket of stars
where wild things grow
in an unlikely instant

With barely a heartbeat
not even a flutter
angel wings were given
and a tiny heart was born
so close to our bed

I carried our love
in my womb
and each contraction a true testament
to the grief my body felt

Tiny wings fluttering
like a hummingbird
barely there and yet now
we did not even know

And you held me so tight
made me feel so safe
as I recovered from screaming
and almost drowning
under dark water of disbelief

You held me so tight and close
as warm fluids spilled down my legs
after a conscious dream
and I finally felt the tissue released

Hemispheres

Halfway across hemispheres I was moved

Halfway across hemispheres I fled

Now watch me grow

Traumatized

I am here
and I am not
I see my body move
and I do not feel my teeth
biting down on my hand

I am here
and so far away
become reactive
terrified

At the core
happy to the bone
safe
a whole new world of wonder
explodes in prisms in front of my eyes
and rainbows of stars
dance on my eyelids

To the bone happy
and yet so traumatized
as I dissociate
in the safest arms I know

Hot tears spill onto my worktable
creating small puddles
of warm salty pain
inhuman deep howls escape my lips
as I struggle for air

I cannot I cannot
I cannot I cannot

To the bones happy
so in love
and I am still so traumatized
I dissociate
in the safest arms I know

Maybe because I know
maybe exactly because I know
not just intellectually
maybe because I see
my own pain reflected

So radiant, beautiful, happy
at peace in my own skin

And yet
I dissociate in your arms

Neuroplasticity

I see the dark wave
as it crashes down on me

Filling my lungs
with burning salt water
and as I look up
the sky is bright and blue

Like stepping through curtains
I am the same
and yet I am not

Exposure therapy on steroids
boundaries being set
and kept
seeing through games
and efforts of manipulation

And all of a sudden
I have diamonds around my neck
all of a sudden
I bear a visual symbol
and very proudly so

Traditions change
and become new
intertwined with
laced slowly with
new meanings

Maybe my traditions
are all I have

And another wave
almost strikes me down
but I have learnt
to thread water
and Writer's Tears
fill my blood

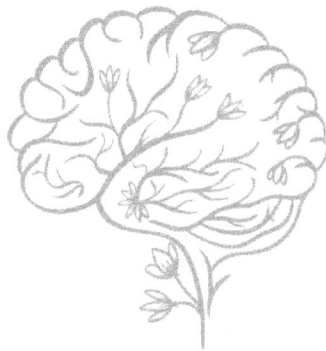

There is a constant flow
a constant movement
a new length, a new wave
as neuroplasticity is allowed to reign

New connections
new workings and habits
the potential
a complete rewiring
clearly showcased in 13-year-old photos
with eyes dark
almost empty
smiling on command

I stare at that photo
no longer recognizing the girl
knowing she is me
and I see no resemblance
except she wears
my face

A once upon a time
a once upon a while
she no longer is
she no longer exists

Co-existing with a brain damage
I never wanted
co-existing with consequences
and conditions
is allowing me a chance
to change in a uniquely
profound manner
a way I never even
dreamt of

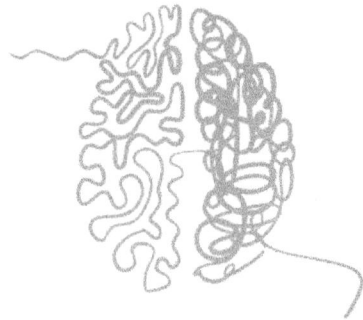

Peace In Pieces

I feel my heart beating
fast, fast, faster
as I notice more

My nerves fire in the dark
shorting the circuit

I try to breathe
as my hands start to tremble
and I hide them
in each other

I just wanted to be divorced
it was never meant to cost
this much

Pulling all the stops
to keep me reigned in
tied to

And I gasp for air
as lyrics allow me to breathe
just for a
second

I just wanted to be done
be left in peace
not in pieces

Quoting statistics I never wanted
to know
seven times on average
this is my final time

And I am so close
I just want to be free
in the arms that are mine
to seek

Avalanche

Something shifted
like the slowest and quietest
avalanche
something shifted
in such a magnanimous capacity
that I felt it deep inside

Something shifted even before
I felt it deep within my body
a reverberating sound
leaving its mark in my skull

I felt it
way before I heard it
your words
a perfect confirmation
of what I was sensing

And it is like I said in July
with you
I feel it all
and then I learn
to find my words

The incremental shift
from "if" to "when"
because it eliminates the uncertainty
so why would I still be weighing
everything
when all I want
is right there

Healing is so hard
it is so hard breaking patterns
and clearly communicating
what I believe I deserve
while it feels we are always
running against the clock

It is an ice-cold shock to the system
a sense of unease
strangeness
and everything feels familiarly foreign

Intense feelings
almost visceral of wanting to
needing to
having to flee
run, run far away

And then I know
and I know nothing
least of all
I do not understand
why I feel the need to run, flee
from someone so good

The closer we get
the stronger the urge in the moment
is it because I am vulnerable?
More than ever?

I fight so intensely
to not run
to not flee
and in turn
my mind triple-guesses everything
and down the rabbit hole I go
red pill or blue pill, miss?

CROSSROADS

Discomfort

Is it me
or is it you
did function become dysfunction?

Snowflakes fall covering
the frozen ground in a blanket
of a thousand diamonds

My hair whip around my face
in the wind
freezing tears in my eyes

And I wonder
if a part of you is looking
for a reason
or if I am
because I don't want
to feel like this anymore

So I sit with the discomfort
of figuring out my emotions
wondering if
you are slowly
disappearing
from my future

Tattoos

Standing at crossroads
everywhere I look

With no elements of clarity
I breathe in
and try to still
my mind

Wish someone would tell me
what to do
because the right thing
and the easy thing
rarely are the same

Have courage
to believe
black words etched
into my skin

My love
do I let go of you?
6 weeks in
I knew I love you
a few more weeks
no questions in my mind
that you are
the one
and I might have to walk away

My children
born of something so dark
and terrible
only children
so good and pure at heart
And I keep stumbling
perpetually coming up
short
and I cannot see you
because pain blinds me
I would give you the world

and it is not me

I stand at crossroads
no matter where I look
and my feet are already
walking them

Like everything was meant to
work out on its own
in its own time

Waitākere

Openly, closed off
fighting intensely
accepting that

---

3 years ago
I wrote kia kaha
3 years ago
is right now
so long ago
and then I am no longer here
I am driving on roads
in Waitākere

3 years ago
came back with a vengeance
kicked my legs out
and while bleeding

It was not
and it is
concurrent
and I try to pivot

No one protected me
and your arms have let me find
a protected space
to safely let me
steer through

Realizing a full
spectrum of emotions
heaving and moving
crashing and colliding
as I find my equilibrium

I fear I almost
lost my marbles
I think I saw
the self-destruction

of a brain unknown
and I am glad
I managed to correct course
3 years ago is a rooting in guilt
and shame
it was humble pie served in...
inhumane lessons
I was unprotected
and I never thought this would happen
I had no crystal ball
at all

So I thought
when I thought of crossroads
it was not this

Me actively walking a different path
than I did
3 years ago
me actively pivoting
into your safe arms
as so often before

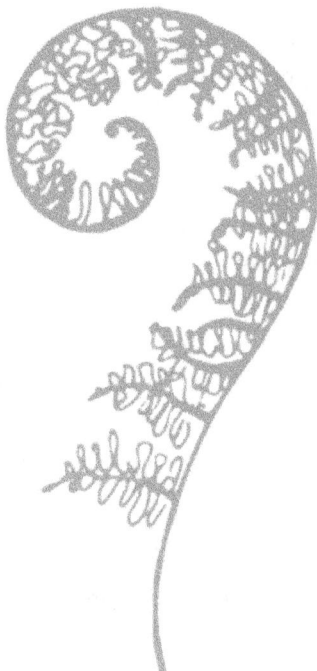

Not Broken

My house is on fire
and the pipes frozen solid
the walls have stories
and they are mute

I am on fire
ablaze with nothing burning
from the inside
as I bleed
drip drop drops
wherever I go

The walls are silent
and the paper in tatters
the windows endless mirrors
of a world beyond
the door revolving
on creaky hinges
and it seems
unaware of being aflame

The house is on fire
my kitchen burning
my bathroom flooding
my house is on fire
yet the walls do not speak
of what they heard
what they saw
and I walk through the fames
staring at words and stories
coming to life before me

No circuit shorted
I was on fire
right ablaze
and I speak
of what I saw
what I heard
and I laugh

Not broken
perfectly imperfect
traumatized
and healing

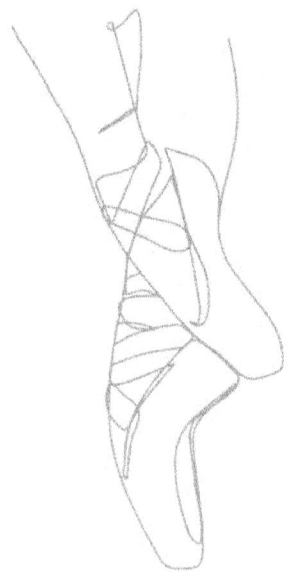

Library

There are books on my shelves
tales I remember
of who I thought
I were
of what I thought
I did

There are parts I grieve
no tears ever shed
there are ideas
of what I want
and I have no idea
if these are things
I no longer can

I lost my sharpest edges
with my smiles
I lost my pointiness
when I started fighting
for myself
I became softer
when I learned
I have worth

Softer, stronger, open
and I keep telling my words
and I let them flow

And with each kiss
you show me a world of glitter
and pink

Rape

I remember how analgesics
needed to be timed
planned
I figured it was my body
I figured that pain
had to be part of it

Lust disappeared
no spontaneity
because pain took over
and so I thought
that sex just was not for me

Until I learned
what safety is
and that safety is
necessary
and never had I thought
I was sleeping with danger
next to me
never had I figured that
sex is consensual
and my consent
never was given

And I stare at the tapestry
of my words
understanding that
pulling this string
will make it so clear
that it was not sex

It was rape

Home

I stopped listening for
the sound your car makes
when it locks

I stopped hoping that sound
meant you through
my front door
and me in your arms

I did not even know
months have gone by
and it seems I now listen
for that same sound
at your place
waiting for you
to come home after a long day

It has been months
since I was T-appropriate
with you
surrounded by the walls
that are meant to be
my home

I do not think it is anymore
maybe
I think we are just slow
to realize
or maybe
mature about it

Affidavits

I have 100s of pages
black on white
emptying my cartridges over
and over
causing queues
and endless printer jobs

Yet they are all fax
no printer
I spent 18 hours deep diving
into text in texts
messages I once understood
that are now nonsensical

I walk on carpets my feet never
should have touched
and I ask permission to speak
freely
my work is meticulous
and a far bigger burden
than anyone should ever
carry

I wait for deadlines
that pass
and answers that
set the gas-a-light
and as I dissociate
and as my body remembers
what my mind cannot
I slip in my mind
and there is no air
my ears are ringing
and while I chant
that my reaction is
proportionate and appropriate
I struggle to embrace and space
that my reaction is
not an overreaction

And I prepare
comparing statements
with statements
finding only untruths
and no accountability
and as I grapple with
a new step
after abuse
I find myself so safe
where hands steady
and it still feels
like coming up for fresh air
where hearts still
skip a beat
or 1.75
where 18 hours are
but a second
and not a circle
of Hell

#NotOkay

As I took the stand
I had no idea
that I would leave
less whole than when I came

I might have won
and I lost a part of myself
words were taken
erased and stolen
not just from me
from the survivors
who came before me
the survivors
who will come after me
from those brave enough
to stay silent no more

My story was untold
made unclaimed
and my children's words
stolen

I lost something in that courtroom
my voice
my words
my reality
my story

Retraumatized

Without knowing
without fully understanding
tears flowed and deep sobs
escaped my lips
only to be replaced
by a comatose sleep

I lost something
and I thought it was the stand
the room
the Justice
or the lack thereof
claiming a part of me
I cannot yet identify
maybe I do not
want to

I thought it was that
not fully understanding
that my mind was
and is working
to protect me
and I keep repeating my words
almost as though I try
to reclaim them
almost as though I try
to make sense of
the nonsensical
almost as though I try
to understand them

I was physically abused
with shivers down my spine
and I feel stuck on that
it keeps repeating itself
as in a loop

I was physically abused
I was struck
by my ~~spouse~~ ex

and the exhaustion
takes over my body

as I reflect, ponder, ruminate
and it slowly dawns on me
that it was not the stand
that I was retraumatized
traumatized yet again
and I realize
I am not stuck, not broken
just fragile and healing

365 Days

For the longest time
I had no idea
I thought I was bleeding ink
onto papers
black on white
and I probably did
except the words
were not mine

And it has been 365 days
and it still feels like
coming up for fresh air
except now I know
I was drowning

And it has been 370 days
since I put pen to paper
and found that my ink
is full of glitter and pink
since I started reclaiming
all the words that were
mine to speak all along

Your soft kisses
on my lips and skin
your hand so firmly
yet gently in mine
as I feel so deeply
a sense of joy
I never truly knew
even existed

And I ponder the coexistence
of a diorama
a true kaleidoscope
of an emotional bloom
where things remain true
all at the same time

I feel it

I feel it all now
how safe I am
where I cannot be found
how much I fight
for my story
and my words
I feel it all
such big feelings
for such a tiny being

And it still feels like
coming up for fresh air
you still feel like
coming up for fresh air
except now I know
I know I truly was drowning
and in your arms
is a home, a space, an embrace
I never could have imagined

And in my heart is a love
for you
I never would have even
dreamed of

Real

Somehow you are still here
somehow I have not left
although I might have tried
although my head told me to

Somehow you are still here
and I woke up next to you
my pillow lives in our bed
somehow you are
actually real
I almost want to pinch myself
this is surely a dream

I grapple at, with
the realization that this
is not a dream
this is my reality
and I find I cannot
stop gushing
because somehow
while I find my words
I believe you are not
too good to be true

Truly remarkable
I validate you
and you find me
through the haze and fog
and bring me safely to shore

Your steady presence
slowly guides me
when you embrace me
and hold the space for me
that I in the moment cannot
hold for myself

I never knew a world
outside of books
I never knew of free choices

made to be with each other
and it is a new kind of
magic

And so I pinch myself
because you are so good
giving me more
than I could ever hope for
my safe in a world of sharps
and you are mine to kiss
and I yours to hold
even in the moments
where I struggle to believe
that you truly are true
even as my fingertips
trace your skin

Insecure

I get insecure
and all of a sudden
everything is questioned

Do not ask where I would
run to
I have no idea
maybe places I do not feel
and am not safe
ask what makes me want
to run

I do not want to discredit you
make you feel anything less
than loved and treasured
and all of a sudden
it feels like all I do
is making pivot upon pivot
in my mind

Everything is double-shook
second-guessed
until it is to the power of ten
everything is mirrored
in a new reflection
and roads split in the infinite
my head spins
and makes up scenarios
that I do not know
the truth of
and I get insecure
and lose my footing

It feels like I stumble
forward
not knowing where
to place my feet or
my hands
is it the same
for you?

do I sometimes make
you insecure?

It becomes so clear
that despite our closeness
our ability to communicate
that we are not the same mind
I am not a mind reader

And I am so terrified
of losing you

Mother's Day

For the second time
you bring me flowers
on Mother's Day
the first time as a
complete surprise
and the second time
with my child
on your arm

As the only one
you have acknowledged
the responsibility I bear
the mother in me
and you take care of
and mind her
too

A Sea Smaller Than Myself

May became June
and June became November
and before I knew
I had trotted through carpeted hallways
for a full year
before I knew
I had been in your arms
for a full year

I did not know
that these crossroads
could be so many
in your shower I sing
the words from Banners
like I did with tears
running down my face
in my own basement
that I could barely be in
not even six months ago
because I truly never believed
that I could swim
so I continued to sink
in a sea smaller than myself

And somehow you saw
a light in me
and believed in me
and I knew I was drowning
now I know
now I understand
and in so many large
and tiny infinities
you are still
like coming up for fresh air
always

And as I place barriers
and orders between myself and
words that no longer define me
words that never did define me

I find a home in our bed
in a house at an address
that is not for me
to call home
I had never expected
the crossroads to be this many
at once

While pieces of me fall behind
in rooms with galleries
and I walk across carpeted hallways
in inches high heels
I walk across and through
an unwelcoming world
clearly stating
I do not belong
and some how we are so
imperfectly perfect
so unbrokenly broken
that my pieces fit
so perfectly with yours
and I would never change this
in a world where I sink
from inexperience
and intimidation
you cheer me on
making me welcome
like I belong
in the house we are not creating
and still
time is ticking

Sorrow

I guess crossroads happen
before any of us really know
so while we talk about a future
no one knew
it would be plurals
or will it?

So am I packing up and leaving my key
when I still believe you might be
my full stop
because you talk about boundaries
and them being crossed
and I never meant to
that is never what I wanted to
because you only told me
of the boundary
once it was too late
can we walk it back
and do we want to
do you still want me?

I am not a mind reader
and I have tried to be
so clear
in my communication
and perhaps you stayed silent
because I see that you are
still stuck
and I hear you
I just do not know
how I can help you
or if you want to be helped
I do not know if this is you
being self-destructive
but I have seen it
for weeks

Snow turned to rain
frost to dampness on the grass
and what I was crying soft and

harsh tears about 2.5 months ago
now seems to be true

and if that is it
I will walk away
knowing that for a year
you truly were
the biggest present
I could have ever asked for
and you no doubt were
like coming up for fresh air
except I am not drowning
anymore

And yet you are not kicking me out

Stoney

Are you okay
as I lap Stoney twice
are you okay
as I stand mute at the island
it looks like you cried
as I look at you with puffy eyelids
what are you going to do
if only I knew
because I do not know anymore
I did not kick you out
you say
and I do not know what you did
then
because we are meant to talk
and you hold me so tight
kissing my forehead once, twice
letting me rinse off
in your shower
as I silently wait for our talk
I am a little mad at you
because I gave you the space
afforded you the grace

And you chose to ignore it

Pivot

And I pack up
your arms still around me
sitting on your bedroom floor
cleaning and organizing
keeping my key
I do not need you in my life
I want you
I long for you
and sharing my life with you
makes all the heavy
so much lighter
I read you
I listen to you
I hear you
and for all my Pisces
aloof and head in the sky
sometimes I do believe
there is lead in my feet
I do not know
if I am too close
or too far away
if I am staring blindly
at an abyss
so I pack up
Keeping my drawers full
and I call bullshit
because you cannot know
what you do not know
I will stay fluffy
you stay solid
and nothing is linear
so we shall pivot
hand in hand
let us catch up
know that I am in

I would marry you in a heartbeat
be so proud to be your wife

HOMECOMING/BREATHING

Anger

This is what I did not want happening.

In flowered minds I try to find an escape from my thoughts that keep running in circles.
Analysis upon analysis, thought after thought that I mostly long for you to say that we should stay.
I tried to escape this hell, I wanted to avoid this with a heightened mind, and instead the waves keep on crashing over me as I roll in its tide. Our tide.
Right now I want to slam the door in your face, and I almost will your name to appear on my phone.
Right now I want to fall to pieces, and I do not know if those are yours to pick up.
Right now I hurt, and I am feeling no pain.
I do not want to talk to you, and I want to tell you all about my day, I want to hear your voice all night.
With headphones in a quiet world. Shielded from the world in a hope that the mind is muted. This feels like so much, too much.
Mostly I hope you tell me to come back. Most I hope you just text me. I need to know you are there.
Back to where I feel unsafe. No matter the papers in place. I will never be safe here. I am not safe here despite lawful restraints.
Did this wound us both? Is there space for each other in healing that?
Did we move in just to move out?
Singing loudly to tune out the thoughts of bewilderment. I feel empty. And I know I am whole.
I guess I hope you miss me.
And I have to feel it all.

Mostly I wish you would knock on my door, and wrap me in your arms.

Permanence

I had not planned to write a book. I never knew that in a year I would write more than 300 pages alone. I did not know I would be writing a book for you of love letters and tales of feelings and growth, and I sigh as I stare at my endless words falling from my pen spilling onto paper.

~~What if there is no consequence for trying?~~
No consequence from figuring things out. What if that was reality? And that trying enabled us to find the right path. What if we learn who and what we are instead of always assuming we know?
All I know now is that I am breathing.

I am not hating you, so very, very far from. I got mad at you for the first time, learned what frustrated with you and mad at you looks like. Learned that fleeting emotions feel different from the staying ones.
Like the difference between thunder and the flowing river.

You ask me if I am okay. I keep saying "fine" because I do not know how to answer that question. Am I meant to answer it at all, and is there any answer that would fully cover it?
There are questions in my head I cannot answer.
You have to do that.

Having mad anger run through me allowed me to grasp an idea of how deeply my feelings for you run.
You know, if this book was not telling enough ♥

Belonging

I could spend half an hour
showing you how fond
my lips are of you
tracing patterns on your soft skin
with my fingertips

I could spend half an hour
just tasting you
memorizing you in my mind
as your warm hands
rest on my waist

I could spend lost
minutes, seconds, infinities
looking into your
beautiful eyes
sensing the heartbeat
from your chest

I could spend eternity
nakedly wrapped up
in your arms
moving to your own
rhythm, pace, and weight

I could spend infinite moments
thinking of you
in my hands
me in yours
and you in me
your hands never leaving
my skin
firmly letting me know
where I belong

Wildfire

Beyond chemistry and shared values
this week has been wild
understanding things from only
my own experience
forgetting to ask how
and jumping to conclusions

Listening and sitting down
with the discomfort
allowing emotions to
move, flow, glow
trying to find a meaning
a sense in analysis
upon analysis

And that is how I know
that what I feel for you
is so true, so real, so pure
because I know how easily
anger and madness consume
I know how it spreads
like a wildfire through dry woods
and there was nothing in my mind
to feed it
so I allowed it to eat
consume the oxygen
it is not that I am blind

I think I just
accept you, love you, treasure you
as you are
without any wishes
or desires
to change you

Vulnerable

That is all I know
all I know is that you
are like coming up
for fresh air
no matter if I am drowning
or not
your kisses are like the
subzero pure mountain air

My head feels like
it is spinning
from nights
in a bed
that should be mine
in a house
that should be mine
and it feels so far from
because the walls are covered
with my pent-up words
and shame
a storm went through here

I try to tell myself I am safe
and it is so clear
that my body knows
the difference now
between what is safe
and what is not
and it feels like I am
almost hungering to be
in your arms

I am so confused
so utterly bewildered
at my ability to be
vulnerable with you
to let you in
my willingness to allow you
all the way in

Because I now have papers
that a storm went through me
and logic would dictate
that I should be
shut off, shut down, shut away

Instead I find a true kaleidoscope
of glitters and pink
and feelings of fluff
I never even knew could exist
and a slow smile on my lips
as I understand
what confidence is

For me
as myself
and with your hand
in mine

Oceans

I tasted the salt on my lips
skinny dipping in lakes
jumping head first into Greek waters
snorkeling in deeper
than dark water in Thailand

Born out of water
with my head in the skies
I find peace in water

Never as a kid would I imagine
dipping my toes in the Pacific
on New Year's Day
staring across two seas colliding
I had no clue
that I would feel so at home
in the salty embrace of
the Adriatic and Mediterranean seas
dipping my toes in the Atlantic
off the Scottish coast
staring into the distance
where ocean and sky become one

Landlocked for almost
twenty-four months
in the foothills on the prairie
never have I been further
from an ocean

Staring at those seas colliding
I had never imagined
I would be fleeing across oceans
putting so many
kilometers, hours, liters
between the very thing
that caused my PTSD

A brain damage I did not know
would happen
a memory wipe so complete

I do not even remember
staring at the colliding seas
of Kattegat and Skagerrak
so many years ago
I just knew I did
I just know I have

And now my bath
is the closest
I get to a full body
warm embrace

Gaslighting

I keep thinking
that I do not abuse myself
because I know
what that looks like
right?

You remarked so clearly
so very early
how adamant I am
in speaking nicely
about myself

So why is it then
that I continue to
gaslight myself so hard
gaslighting is
a form of abuse
right?

Abuse

He threatened to kill me
to wring my neck
stab me in the neck
with scissors

He threatened with
homicide, infanticide, and suicide
or maybe it was promises
all along

He told me mercy
would be killing me first
so I would not have
to witness
my children dying

He reiterated this
in front of medical personnel
in different countries
and I was so used
to hearing those words
so used I did not compute
that the risk was real

He told me
he would make me
shut up
have a toilet shoved
up ~~my~~ where my kids
were born from
and he struck me
across my face

I had always thought
that would be a hard boundary for me
and he stepped over it
invaded my mind
penetrated my boundaries
and I feel so unsafe

For years he leveraged threats
of injury and death
as bargaining chips
over me
accusing me
of sleeping with others
as soon as
I was out of view

I was a player in a game
where the rules
changed constantly
and where callous disregard
was dished out
as a serving of love

I always said I did not
want to become a warzone
interpreter
because I knew my mind
could not withstand
those experiences
that environment

Little did I know
I was mediating a warzone
at home
trying to mitigate
and put out fires
little did I know
I had married someone
that would put me at odds
where I would have to flee
to stay alive

Safe Spaces

I am so in love with you
and the version of me
that I am able to explore
in the safe spaces
you provide for me

I did not know it
and I was drowning
and in your arms
I am more than just head
above water
like coming up for
fresh air

I am so in love with you
and the foundation, space
grace and patience
we hold for each other
unexpectedly, consistently

I am getting to know myself
I am learning
a work in progress
as I start to remember things
that I forgot or repressed
decades ago
like taking your clothes off
because they are too heavy in water

And now I feel things
I have never felt before
deeply, highly sensitively
feelings of devotion, love, wonder

I do not think I ever
really knew what love is
I always thought
to look for butterflies
and when they left
it was bad

I do not think I understood
that love and fear
do not belong together

And all I know now
is that I am twirling
in this space
that is ours
keeping these
unpredictably found
unexpectedly discovered
feelings preciously
cared for

And that I am not as lost
as I am found
no longer alienated
as much as belonging
and that serenity feels
like the smell of rain

I was drowning for years
and now somehow
I am not
remembering things
Instead of finding
empty spaces
I was drowning for years
and I am so in love with you
and what I am becoming

Waiting

I am waiting
in the middle of the storm
drenched
soaked to the bone
I am waiting
for this storm
to dry up

I am feeling things
I have no idea how to feel
and I understand
on a level
that is intellectually new

Terrified, stunned, horrified
trying to prepare
almost dissociating
one step away from
picking unnecessary fights
I am sorry
backing away so I protect
us both
as I try to pivot
through what this next date
is bringing up

I am standing
drenched on the street
in the middle of a storm
I never wanted
waiting for the storm
to run out of rain

Your Honor

In 96 hours I will walk
across carpet I have seen
too many times
into a room that stripped me down
into a room
where I was left unprotected

I filed a complaint
taking back my words
claiming what is rightfully mine
to claim and own
It feels like
I am alight with shame

Terrified for what
I will find in my inbox
tomorrow
I want to run away
because once again
I feel like Atlas
with the world and its pain
on my frail shoulders

I have been waiting
for the moment I would be free
one signature and 31 days
is all it takes
and all legal ties are severed

I could have been free now
I should have been free now
I was thinking
that my freedom would make
the task easier
the load lighter

Instead I have to walk across
muted halls
next to silently listening walls
stating that my marriage

caused me to develop
a brain damage
and it feels like all my synapses
misfire at once
I am alight with
shame, sorrow, and fury

I was a person
I am a person
and 1825 days ago
I left a country that was never home
only to be trapped by
false promises
I am not broken, in repair
my marriage resulted in
a brain damage
and now I must speak those words
in court
Your Honor

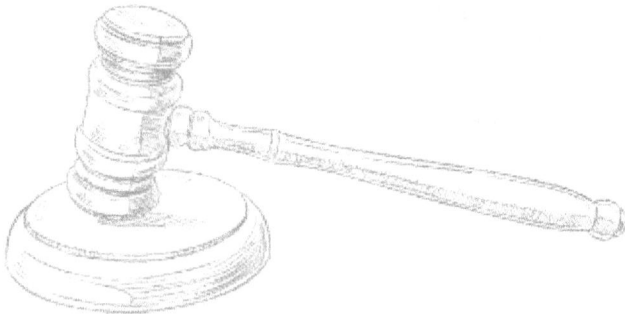

FALLING/SUICIDE

SHE REMEMBERED THE NEEDLES, the braids, the pain, the scars and the rewritings of a life, which in so many ways, was already broken into a thousand pieces. She remembered the screams and apologies; the insults and downfalls, which trumped every tiny victory. The naked skin reacting with every caress from the naked steel. The drops from the orange smelling so sweet before it became vitamins and stuffing in her empty stomach. A single kiss. Oh, how she wanted to... taste the forbidden fruit again, just once before the steel would steal her life.

HE LAID HER ONTO the table. She couldn't do anything, but it wasn't the first time. His eyes were thunder and lightning from unknown eager. It scared her. Hands felt their way up her thighs, under her dress. With them followed her panties. The fingers were warm when they found their way up her dress once again. Carefully they fondled her. She covered her eyes with her hands. A metallic taste dominated her mouth. She heard the belt rattle. When she peaked through her fingers, she saw him stand up. She did not make a sound, because he would hit her. He took her hips. She bit her tongue; her hips were sore. Underneath the skin blue violets were spreading, and she did not know how to explain. She was not clumsy, but somehow, she had fallen.

She was thin. Skinny even, beyond explanation. She looked at the dish in front of her. Her stomach growled on cue, but the hand did not touch the fork. They really had outdone themselves when they had cooked for her; pasta with cartoon figures and small pieces of chicken, which would stuff her. Bloat her like a balloon. She could win, she had to win. If she gave in everything would be lost. If everything was lost, what mattered anymore? The finger played with the cold steel. In a minute they would grab ahold. Then she would lose. She opened her mouth and chewed mechanically. She did it by heart. On the other side of the table, curios eyes looked at her, sparkling from optimism. She could throw up. The stomach hurt, but she kept eating. Until the plate was as empty as it had been before the food.

IN THIS MOMENT THERE was no doubt. The band played and she let his hand explore the body that was closer to being a woman than being a kid. Rainbow flowers bloomed across her eyelids and warmth spread through her body like a river breaking the last ice of the winter. Loving feelings crashed through her when he kissed her ear. She raised her arm, caressing him softly on the neck. He saw a girl who was fighting the stage lights for sparkles-and there was no doubt who won. She felt happiness and safety so strongly that there were only those two. Mixed emotions crushed her as a wave when he kissed the corner of her mouth. Fireworks exploded in her vision. They were the only two, and no one else. Dizzy from happiness she turned her head. In that moment she felt a complete wholeness as he carefully kissed her lips with a passion she had not ever experienced. Heat, cold and happiness against pain met in a thunderstorm and radiated throughout her body. In that moment there was no doubt at all. She let go and fell.

THE COLD STEEL DANCED on her lower arms and drew red lines. The pain was simple. Focus removing, killing and oddly oxygen giving. There was always something calming about the red color. Such a deep red, thick and beautiful. The drops were the prettiest. As they artistically let go of the alabaster skin and fell to the cloth underneath. It was unbelievable that one sharp blade could cause so much absolute beauty. Pure beauty, untainted by damage and cracks. She saw the blush spread as a rose underneath the skin, and she looked at her masterpiece with pride. For long she would sit while the blood would dry out and stiffen. Some places the skin would raise up in angry protest against the art she painted onto it, but she did not care. The control was hers; the rest did not matter.

QUIET TEARS, SO SILENTLY they fell. The lip was quivering slightly, but she did not dare to give in. The hits were falling all around her. She felt how the beating was stealing the breath from her lungs. Could she be put more under?
The pain was a lightning shooting through her. Her eyes blackened when her cheek received a hand. The yells imprinted on her eyes and the angry face created nightmares instead of good dreams. She never quite understood it, she never quite got around to understanding it. Blood spread out through her mouth, but she did not feel the pain from her tongue where she had bit down. Her conscience was hanging by a thread. Her legs gave way. She never did understand. She was never the one who fell off her bike on the way home from school, yet she had fallen. Falling... now she only fell in the darkness.

THERE WAS NO ORDER in her mess. There was a mess in her order. It was not her fault! There were messes everywhere, nothing made sense! A thought would grow inside of her, and she would make it go away. It would never be possible. From the mirror a healthy girl stared back. Could she take control of her own life? Now others had taken control of it. She could do it by herself. She would do it. The thought won through. It grew in her and grew strong. The thought won ground. Before long the thought was her life. She had the strength. It was hidden underneath many layers, but she found it. She lit a fire, and she burned herself, but she continued onwards as she had before, only down a completely different path. There needed to be order in her mess. Because messes can be tamed.

HE HELD HER HAND. He held her close. She felt a safety she could not comprehend, and she stiffened. She knew it was wrong. Wrong! So very attractive, so very right. She could feel her heartbeat behind the protective cage of ribs. She could feel his heartbeat against hers. Without words or actions, he reached for her, and she caught on. Slowly, so tryingly she reached towards him as well as she could. Infinitesimally softly he embraced her with all his being. It was as if he sensed what she needed. It was as if he sensed that she was just a piece of porcelain. She

104

could not help but wonder if he could see all the cracks that had been made. Did he see the wholeness or just the glue, keeping it together? She felt happy. Happy, in love and relaxed. Now she would not be alone in her fall. They fell together. Together. For ever. Forever falling together, hand in hand. Together...

IT WAS NOT DIFFICULT to flee to another dimension in another world. When she was on the plane she imagined she would be on her way to a different destination. Sometimes she imagined she was riding on elephants in Thailand. It was another world to her because she knew she would never go to Thailand. It was always the same places. Mallorca and a single time to Tenerife. It bored her. Always the same hotel, the same staff, the same food and the forced feeling of having to eat. She had the control, but the art was hiding that she had the control. She knew the art was obvious on her arm. She loved symmetry, because order belonged there. It was a complex and extremely simple work that spread throughout her arms. A constant and unchangeable beauty. It was not temporary or relative. It was absolute and constant in her eyes. Like the deep red drops that twirled around her arms and fingers when she painted. It was like walking into a wall. Her alabaster skin was screaming in the sun. Sun. Too much sun. Too much, too little water. Too much sun, too little water. Too little sun, too much water.

RED THREADS FOLLOWED MANY small pathways on the white porcelain. Every little bit helps. She had heard that when she was younger. Silver pieces formed obstacles on the porcelain, and the red threads made their way around. Some were deep red, others pink, thin. She stared into the smashed mirror. The face was twisted into a thousand pieces, the tears had drawn black streaks over the hollowed cheeks. She had the strength! She was brave, the bravest! She could finish. She stared at her hand that stained the sink with blood. There were cuts in it. On the mirror were deep red marks from where she smashed her hand into it.

On one wrist was a tightly woven pattern of white scars, the unchangeable beauty that dominated her world. In nightmares, dreams and daydreams. A couple of morphine tablets lay in front of her, and in the broken hand she had a piece of cold, but very sharp steel. The pills were greedily sucking up the red liquid when she grabbed ahold of them. She let them lie on her tongue and enjoyed the bitter taste. Then she downed them. With strong and determined hands she grabbed the steel as if it was a newborn.
The pain was non-existent. She saw the blood flood down the porcelain only to disappear down the drain. It was beautiful. She saw the beauty, and, in that moment, she cried from happiness. She was never the one to fall, but everything fell from her. She was never the one to fall, but everything in her fell apart. In her mind she let the deep red ocean swallow her, and she knew that she would never fall again.

ABOUT DOMESTIC VIOLENCE

Domestic violence (DV), family violence (FV), intimate partner violence (IPV) are serious matters. It is estimated that 1 in 3 women (WHO, 2024) during their life will experience domestic violence.

Most notably, there is a significant underreporting of domestic violence rooted in a fear of retaliation, stigma, isolation, economic dependence and a lack of available support.

Domestic violence does not discriminate and affects all societal groups, and statistics vary drastically depending on culture and country with New Zealand having the highest rate of domestic violence in the OECD (University of Auckland, 2020), and Canada with a rate of 44% equal to approximately 6.2 million women (Government of Canada, 2022).

It takes on average 7 times to leave an abusive relationship (National Domestic Violence Hotline, 2024), and it is normal to leave and get back together with an abuser several times due to the pervasive cycle of abuse (Rakovec-Felser, 2014).

Leaving an abuser is difficult, and it is incredibly dangerous, and this danger is only increased every time the abuser is left.

9 781068 872518